Walter Crane, Edmund Evans

Triplets

Comprising, The Baby's Opera, The Baby's Bouquet, and The Baby's own Æsop

Walter Crane, Edmund Evans

Triplets

Comprising, The Baby's Opera, The Baby's Bouquet, and The Baby's own Æsop

ISBN/EAN: 9783744751919

Printed in Europe, USA, Canada, Australia, Japan

Cover: Foto ©Thomas Meinert / pixelio.de

More available books at **www.hansebooks.com**

CONTENTS

PREFACE.

THE BABIES who were present when THE BABY'S OPERA had its first season have all grown up, but perhaps the thrilling scene is still remembered when the Cat & the Fiddle were in the orchestra, & everyone in breathless suspense, when the moon rose, waiting to see which way the Cow would jump; though all ended happily in the Little Dog's laughing chorus, during which the Dish seized the opportunity to elope with the Spoon. Anyway it still holds the boards.

The flowers, too, of THE BABY'S BOUQUET are still fresh in the nursery estimation after all these years, while that perennial fount of world-wisdom still flows out of the mouths of babes & sucklings in ÆSOP'S primitive but profound Fables.

Let the first BABY pipe the old tunes again, while the others dance, or let them each & all in turn—like the gifted Bill & Jane in the BAB BALLADS - pipe as well as dance, & let the dear public respond, while that infant ÆSOP who is knocking at the door- brings his wise saws & moral reflections up to date.

If the Nursery Constituency, & its responsible guides,

philosophers & friends have here tofore accepted ... Baby Books singly, may now, it is thought, like them ... & in rather longer clothes than of old, & new ... ers. It is very much a question of the most convenient sort of perambulator, or mail cart, or perhaps motor car with a growing family, & of course it is important to see that none of them fall out.

In the form of TRIPLETS, then our old ... are again respectfully presented, &, with rings on ... & bells on their toes, so to speak, I commend them ... new go-cart to - Banbury Cross, or any other nice ... where cakes are to be had

Walter Crane

Kensington 1899.

THE BABY'S OPERA

A BOOK OF OLD RHYMES WITH NEW DRESSES
BY WALTER CRANE
THE MUSIC BY THE EARLIEST MASTERS

·THE

·BABY'S·OPERA·

·KING·COLE·

THE

·BABY'S·OPERA·

A
BOOK·OF·OLD   THE·MUSIC·BY
RHYMES·WITH   THE·EARLIEST
NEW·DRESSES   M A S T E R S
BY

WALTER · CRANE.
ENGRAVED,&PRINTED IN COLOURS BY E.DMUND EVANS.

TO

THE HONOURABLE

MRS. GEORGE HOWARD.

CONTENTS

20

GIRLS AND BOYS
1. Girls and boys come out to play, The moon doth shine as bright as day; Come with a whoop, and come with a call, Come with a good will or not at all.
2. Leave your sup-per, and leave your sleep, Come to your playfellows in the street; Up the lad-der and down the wall, A pen - ny loaf will serve you all.

THE MVL-BERRY-BVSH

Here we go round the mulberry bush, the mulberry bush, the mulberry bush;

Here we go round the mulberry bush, All on a frosty morning.

This is the way we clap our hands, This is the way we clap our hands,

This is the way we clap our hands, All on a frosty morning.

·HERE·
WE·GO·
·ROVND·
·THE·
·MVLBERRY·
·BVSH·

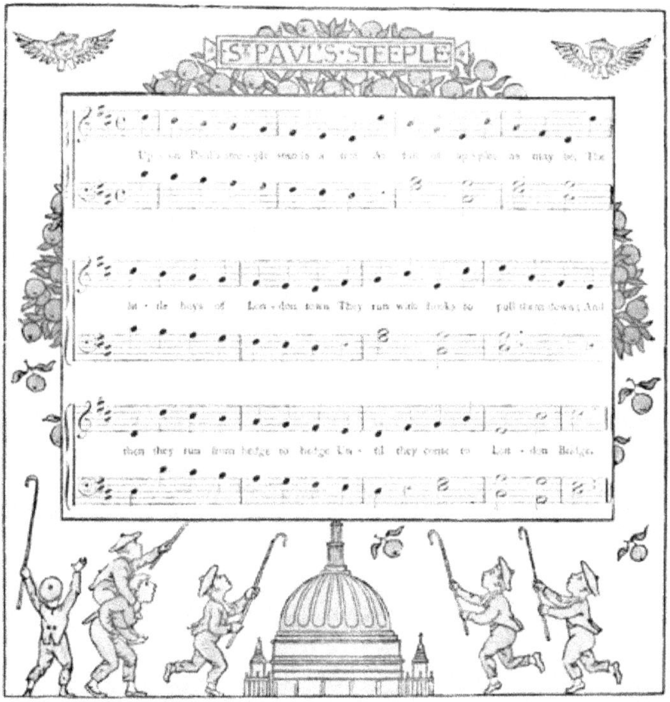
St PAUL'S STEEPLE

MY LA DY'S GAR DEN
How does my la - - dy's gar - den grow? How does my
la - - dy's gar - den grow? With sil - - ver bells, and
coc - kle shells, And pret - ty maids all in a row!.......

·HOW·DOES·
·MY·LADY'S·
·GARDEN·
·GROW·
?

·NATURAL·HISTORY·

1. What are lit-tle boys made of?
2. What are lit-tle girls made of?

What are lit-tle boys made of? Frogs and snails and
What are lit-tle girls made of? Su-gar and spice and

pup-py-dog's tails, And that are lit-tle boys made of.
all that's nice, And that are lit-tle girls made of.

3. What are young men made of?
What are young men made of?
Sighs and leers, and crocodile tears,
And that are young men made of.

4. What are young women made of?
What are young women made of?
Ribbons and laces, and sweet pretty faces,
And that are young women made of.

·LAVENDER'S · BLVE ·

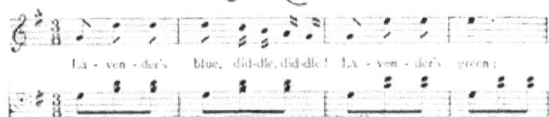

La - ven - der's blue, did-dle, did-dle! La - ven - der's green;

When I am king, did-dle, diddle! You shall be queen.

2 Call up your men, diddle, diddle!
  Set them to work;
  Some to the plough, diddle, diddle!
  Some to the cart.

3 Some to make hay, diddle, diddle!
  Some to cut corn;
  Whilst you and I, diddle, diddle!
  Keep ourselves warm.

I SAW THREE SHIPS

1. I saw three ships come sail - ing by,
2. And what do you think was in them then,

Sail - ing by, sail - ing by, I saw three ships come
In them then, in them then, And what do you think was

sail - ing by, On New-year's Day in the morn - - ing.
in them then, On New-year's Day in the morn - - ing?

3. Three pretty girls were in them then,
   In them then, in them then,
   Three pretty girls were in them then,
   On New-year's Day in the morning.

4. And one could whistle, and one could sing,
   The other play on the violin;
   Such joy there was at my wedding,
   On New-year's Day in the morning.

I·SAW· THREE·SHIPS·

DING·DONG·BELL

Ding dong bell! Pussy's in the well! Who put her in? Lit-tle Tommy Lin.

Who pulled her out? Lit-tle Tommy Stout. What a naughty boy was that To

drown poor pussy-cat, Who ne'er did any harm, But killed all the mice in fa-ther's barn.

· PUSS · AT · COURT ·

"Pussy-cat, pussy-cat, where have you been?"   "I've been to
Lon-don to look at the Queen."   "Pussy-cat, pussy-cat,
what did you there?"   "I caught a lit-tle mouse un-der the chair."

THREE·BLIND·MICE

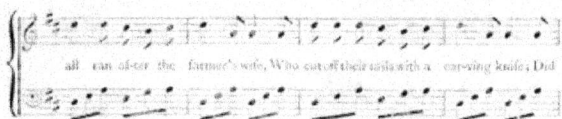

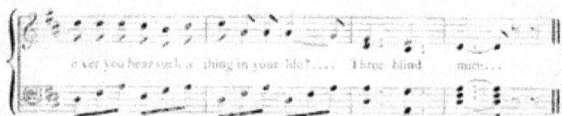

Three blind mice... See how they run! They all ran af-ter the farmer's wife, Who cut off their tails with a carving knife, Did e-ver you hear such a thing in your life?.... Three blind mice...

· DICKORY · DOCK ·

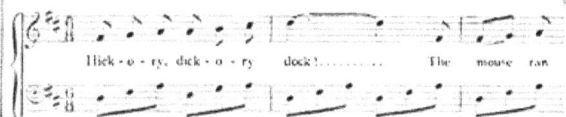

Hick - o - ry, dick - o - ry dock!.......... The mouse ran

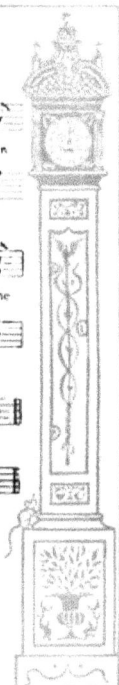

up the clock;.......... The clock struck one, The

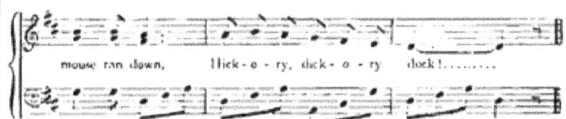

mouse ran down, Hick - o - ry, dick - o - ry dock!........

Y^e FROG'S WOOING

1. It was the frog lived in the well, Heigh-ho! says Row-ley; And the mer-ry mouse un-der the mill, With a Row-ley, Pow-ley, Gammon, and Spinach, Heigh-ho! says Anthony Row-ley.

2.
The frog he would a-wooing ride, Heigholds, &c.
Sword and buckler by his side, With a, &c.

3.
When upon his high horse set, Heighold, &c.
His boots they shone as black as jet, With a, &c.

4.
When he came to the merry mill-pin, Heighold, &c.
"Lady Mouse, are you within?" With a, &c.

5.
Then came out the dusty mouse, Heighold, &c.
"I am the lady of this house," With a, &c.

6.
"Hast thou any mind of me?" Heighold, &c.
"I have e'en great mind of thee," With a, &c.

7.
"Who shall this marriage make?" Heighold, &c.
"Our lord, which is the rat," With a, &c.

8.
"What shall we have to our supper?" Heighold, &c.
"Three beans in a pound of butter," With a, &c.

9.
But when the supper they were at, Heighold, &c.
The frog, the mouse, and even the rat, With a, &c.

10.
Then came in Tib, our cat, Heighold, &c.
And caught the mouse even by the back, With a, &c.

11.
Then did they separate, Heighold, &c.
And the frog leaped on the floor so flat, With a, &c.

12.
Then came in Dick, our drake, Heighold, &c.
And drew the frog even to the lake, With a, &c.

13.
The rat he ran up the wall, Heighold, &c.
And so the company parted all, With a, &c.

Ye FROG & Ye CROW

1. A jol-ly fat frog lived in the ri-ver swim, O! A come-ly black crow lived on the ri-ver brim, O! "Come on shore, come on shore," Said the crow to the frog, and then, O! "No, you'll bite me, no, you'll bite me," Said the frog to the crow a-gain, O!

2. " O ! there is sweet music on yonder green
     hill, O !
   And you shall be a dancer, a dancer in
     yellow,
   All in yellow, all in yellow,"
   Said the crow to the frog, and then, O !
   " All in yellow, all in yellow,"
   Said the frog to the crow again, O !

3. " Farewell, ye little fishes, that in the river
     swim, O !
   I'm going to be a dancer, a dancer in yel-
     low,"
   " O beware ! O beware !"
   Said the fish to the frog, and then, O !
   " I'll take care, I'll take care,"
   Said the frog to the fish again, O !

4. The frog began a swimming, a swimming
     to hand, O !
   And the crow began jumping to give him
     his hand, O !
   " Sir, you're welcome, Sir, you're welcome,"
   Said the crow to the frog, and then, O !
   " Sir, I thank you, Sir, I thank you,"
   Said the frog to the crow, again, O !

5. " But where is the sweet music on yonder
     green hill, O ?
   And where are all the dancers, the dancers
     in yellow ?
   All in yellow, all in yellow ?"
   Said the frog to the crow, and then, O !
   " Sir, they're here, Sir, they're here,"
   Said the crow to the frog—*

     * Here the crow swallows the frog.

MRS BOND

1. "Oh, what have you got for dinner, Mrs. Bond?" "There's beef in the larder, and ducks in the pond;" "Dilly, dilly, dilly, dilly, come to be killed, For you must be stuffed, and my customers filled!"

2. "John Ostler, go fetch me a duckling or two,
John Ostler go fetch me a duckling or two;
Cry dilly, dilly, dilly, dilly, come and be killed,
For you must be stuffed, and my customers filled!"

3. "I have been to the ducks that are swimming in the pond,
And they won't come to be killed, Mrs. Bond;
I cried dilly, dilly, dilly, dilly, come and be killed,
For you must be stuffed, and the customers filled!"

4. Mrs. Bond she went down to the pond in a rage,
With plenty of onions, and plenty of sage;
She cried, "Come, little wag-tails, come, and be killed,
For you shall be stuffed, and my customers filled!"

MRS BOND

XMAS
·DAY·
·IN·Yᵉ·
MORN
·ING·

1. Dame, get up and bake your pies,
   Bake your pies, bake your pies;
   Dame, get up and bake your pies,
   On Christ-mas-day in the morn - - ing.

2. Dame, what makes your maid - ens lie,
   Maid - ens lie, maid - ens lie?
   Dame, what makes your maid - ens lie,
   On Christ-mas-day in the morn - - ing?

3. Dame, what makes your ducks to die,
   Ducks to die, ducks to die?
   Dame, what makes your ducks to die,
   On Christmas-day in the morning?

4. Their wings are cut, they cannot fly,
   Cannot fly, cannot fly;
   Their wings are cut, they cannot fly,
   On Christmas-day in the morning.

·LITTLE·JACK·HORNER·

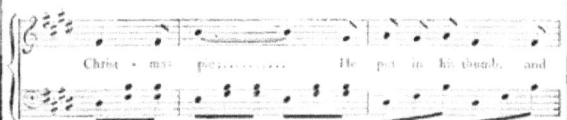

KING ARTHUR

1. When good King Ar-thur ruled this land, He
was a good-ly king— He stole three pecks of
bar-ley-meal, To make a bag pud-ding.

2. A bag pudding the Queen did make,
And stuffed it well with plums,
And in it put great lumps of fat
As big as my two thumbs.

3. The King and Queen did eat thereof,
And noblemen beside,
And what they could not eat that night
The Queen next morning fried.

Ye JOLLY MiLLER

There was a jol-ly mil-ler once Lived on the ri-ver Dee..... He worked and sang from morn till night, No lark more blithe than he....... And this the bur-den of his song For e-ver used to be,...... "I care for no-body, no, not I, And no-body cares for me".....

Yᵉ SONG oF SIXPENCE

1. Sing a song of six - pence, a pocket full of rye; four and twenty

black - birds baked in a pie; When the pie was o - pen the

birds began to sing. Was-n't that a dain-ty dish to set before the king?

The king was in his counting-house counting out his money;
The queen was in the parlour eating bread and honey;
The maid was in the garden hanging out her clothes,
When up came a blackbird and pecked off her nose.

47

1. Lit-tle Bo-Peep, she lost her sheep, And did-n't know where to find them; Let them a-lone, they'll all come home And bring their tails be-hind them.

2. Little Bo-Peep fell fast asleep,
And dreamt she heard them bleating;
But when she awoke, she found it a joke,
For they were still a-fleeting.

3. Then up she took her little crook,
Determined for to find them,
She found them indeed, but it made her heart bleed,
For they'd left their tails behind them.

4. It happened one day as Bo-Peep did stray
Into a meadow hard by,
There she espied their tails side by side,
All hung on a tree to dry.

5. She heaved a sigh and wiped her eye,
Then went o'er hill and dale,
And tried what she could, as a shep-herdess should,
To tack to each sheep its tail.

48

LITTLE
BO·PEEP

"BAA! BAA! BLACK SHEEP"

"Baa! Baa! Black sheep, have you a-ny wool?" "Yes, mar-ry, have I, three bags full: One for my mas-ter, and one for my dame, But none for the lit-tle boy that lives down the lane!"

TOM, THE PIPER'S SON

Tom, Tom, the piper's son, Stole a pig and a-way did run. The

pig was eat, and Tom was beat. And Tom went roar-ing down the street.

THERE WAS A LADY LOVED A SWINE

1. There was a la - dy loved a swine, "Ho - ney!" said she;
2. "I'll build thee a sil - ver sty, Ho - ney!" said she;

"Pig - hog, wilt thou be mine?" "Hunc!" said he.
"And in it thou shalt lie!" "Hunc!" said he.

3. "Pinned with a silver pin,
   Honey!" said she;
   "That thou mayest go out and in."
   "Hunc!" said he.

4. "Will thou have me now,
   Honey?" said she;
   "Speak, or my heart will break."
   "Hunc!" said he.

THERE WAS A LADY LOVED A SWINE

·OVER·THE·HILLS·&·FAR·AWAY·

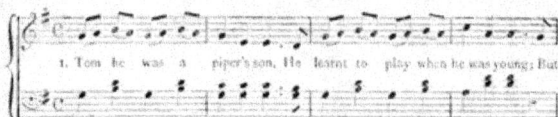

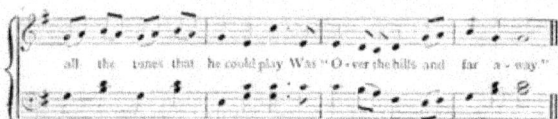

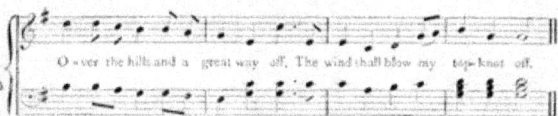

1. Tom he was a piper's son, He learnt to play when he was young; But all the tunes that he could play Was "O·ver the hills and far a·way." O·ver the hills and a great way off, The wind shall blow my top-knot off.

2. Tom with his pipe made such a noise
That he pleased both the girls and boys,
And they stopped to hear him play,
"Over the hills and far away."
    Over the hills, &c.

COCK-ROBIN
JENNY WREN

1. 'Twas on a merry time, When Jenny Wren was young, So neatly as she
2. "My dearest Jenny Wren, If you will but be mine, You shall dine on cherry

danced, And 'twas sweetly as she sung, Robin Redbreast lost his heart, He
pie, And drink nice currant wine; I'll dress you like a goldfinch, Or

was a gallant bird, He doffed his cap to Jenny Wren, Requesting to be heard;
like a peacock gay, So if you'll have me, Jenny, dear, Let us appoint the day."

3. Jenny blush'd behind her fan,   1. Robin Redbreast got up early,
   And thus declared her mind :—   All at the break of day,
   "So let it be tomorrow, Rob,   He flew to Jenny Wren's house,
   " I'll take your offer kind ;   And sang a roundelay :
   " Cherry pie is very good,   He sang of Robin Redbreast,
   " And so is currant wine ;   And pretty Jenny Wren,
   " But I will wear my plain brown gown,   And when he came unto the end,
   " And never dress too fine."   He then began again.

55

I HAD·A·LITTLE· NVT·TREE

I had a lit - tle nut - tree, no - thing would it bear

But a sil-ver nut-meg and a gold-en pear; The King of Spain's daughter

came to vi - sit me, And all for the sake of my lit-tle nut - tree.

I HAD A
LITTLE

NVT
TREE

DR· FAVSTVS

Doc-tor Faus-tus was a good man, He whipt his scho-lars now and then;

When he whipt he made them dance Out of Eng-land in-to France;

Out of France in-to Spain, And then he whips them back a-gain.

·THREE· CHILDREN·

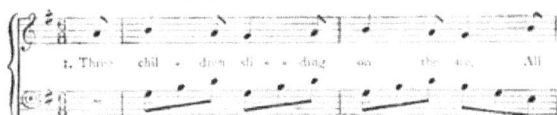

1. Three chil-dren sli-ding on the ice, All on a sum-mer's day........ As it fell out, they all fell in, The rest they ran a-way........

2. Now, had these children been at home,
   Or sliding on dry ground,
   Ten thousand pounds to one penny,
   They had not all been drowned.

3. You parents all that children have,
   And you that have got none,
   If you would have them safe abroad,
   Pray keep them safe at home.

MY·PRETTY·MAID·

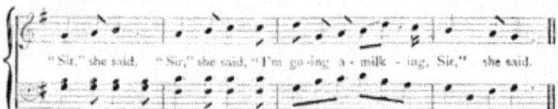

1. "Where are you going to, my pret-ty maid? Where are you going to, my pretty maid?" "I'm go - ing a - milk - ing, Sir," she said.

"Sir," she said, "Sir," she said, "I'm go-ing a - milk - ing, Sir," she said.

2. "Shall I go with you, my pretty maid?"
"Yes, if you please, kind Sir," she said,
"Sir," she said, "Sir," she said,
"Yes, if you please, kind Sir," she said.

3. "What is your fortune, my pretty maid?"
"My face is my fortune, Sir," she said,
"Sir," she said, "Sir," she said,
"My face is my fortune, "Sir," she said.

4. "Then I can't marry you, my pretty maid."
"Nobody asked you, Sir," she said,
"Sir," she said, "Sir," the said,
"Nobody asked you, Sir," she said.

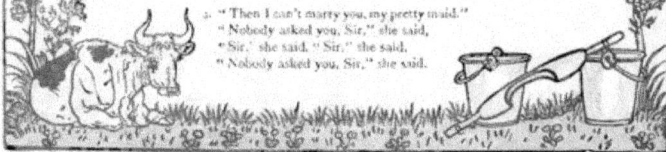

'WHERE ARE YOU
GOING TO MY
PRETTY MAID?'

THE·PLOVGHBOY·IN·LVCK·

1. My dad-dy is dead, but I can't tell you how; He
left me six hor-ses to fol-low the plough: With my whim wham wad-dle ho!
Strim stram strad-dle ho' Bub-ble ho' pret-ty boy, o - ver the brow.

2. I sold my six horses to buy me a cow;
And wasn't that a pretty thing to follow
the plough?   With my, &c.

3. I sold my cow to buy me a calf;
For I never made a bargain but I lost the
best half.   With my, &c.

4. I sold my calf to buy me a cat,
To sit down before the fire so warm her
little back.   With my, &c.

5. I sold my cat to buy me a mouse,
But she took fire in her tail and so burnt
up my house.   With my, &c.

·WARM·HANDS·

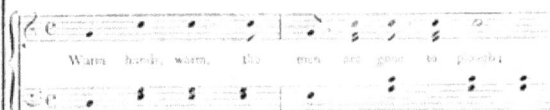

Warm hands, warm, the men are gone to plough;

If you want to warm your hands, warm your hands now.

JACK AND JILL

Jack and Jill went up the hill To fetch a
pail of wa - ter; Jack fell down and
broke his crown, And Jill came tum - bling af - ter.

JACK   86   JILL.

DANCE A BABY

Dance a ba-by did-dy!..... What can
mam-my do wid 'e?..... Sit in her lap,
Give it some pap, And dance a ba-by did-dy!.....

·HVSH-A·BY BABY·

Hush-a-by ba - by on the tree top,   When the wind

blows   the   cra - dle will rock: When the bough breaks   the

cra - dle will fall -   Down comes ba - by cra - dle and all.

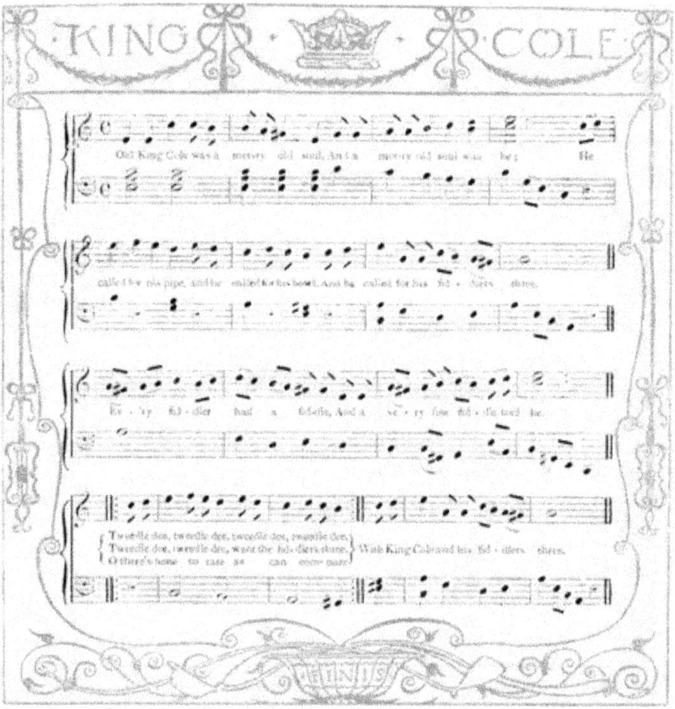
KING · COLE

THE BABY'S BOUQUÊT

A COMPAN'ION' 'TO' THE 'BABY'S' 'OPERA'

A FRESH BUNCH OF OLD RHYMES & TUNES

ARRANGED & DECORATED BY WALTER CRANE

THE BABY'S BOUQUET

CUT & PRINTED IN COLOURS BY E.E.

THE TUNES COLLECTED & ARRANGED BY L.C.

ARRANGED & DECORATED BY
WALTER CRANE

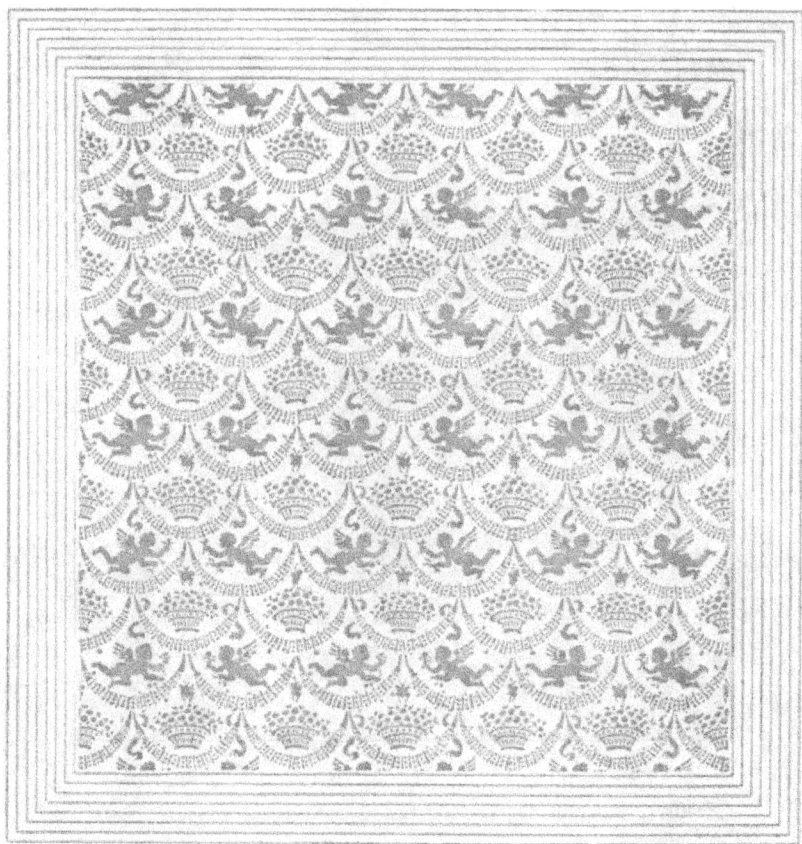

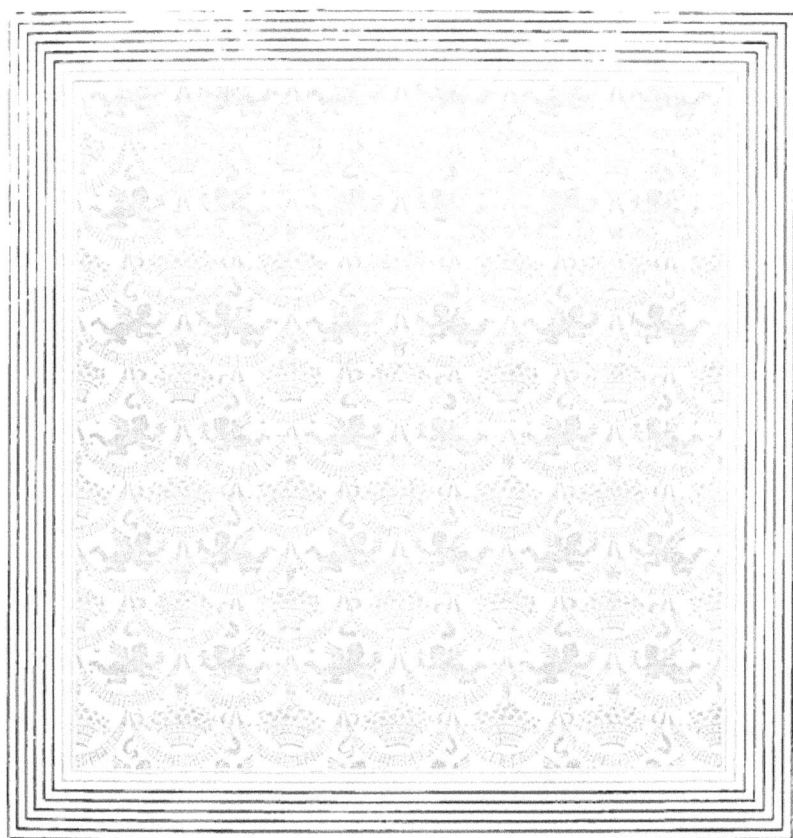

THE
BABY'S BOUQUÊT.

THE BABY'S BOUQUET

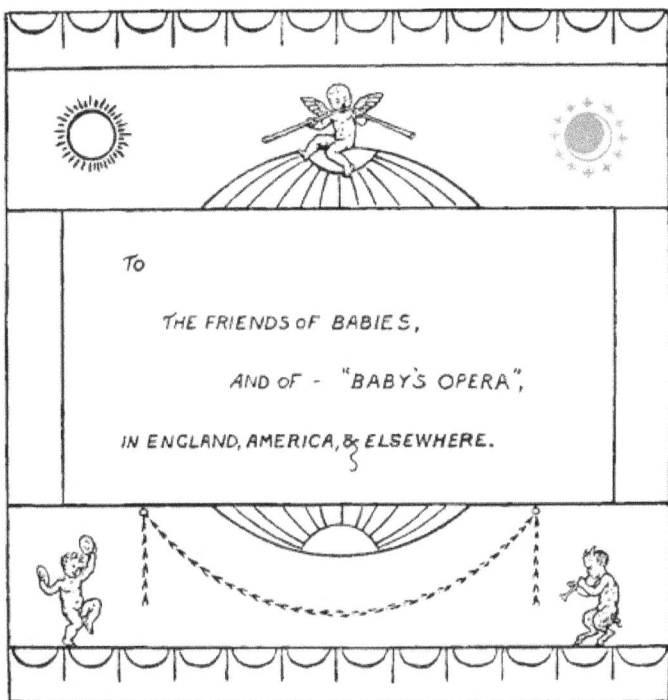

To

THE FRIENDS OF BABIES,

AND OF - "BABY'S OPERA",

IN ENGLAND, AMERICA, & ELSEWHERE.

CONTENTS

POLLY
PUT·THE
KETTLE
ON

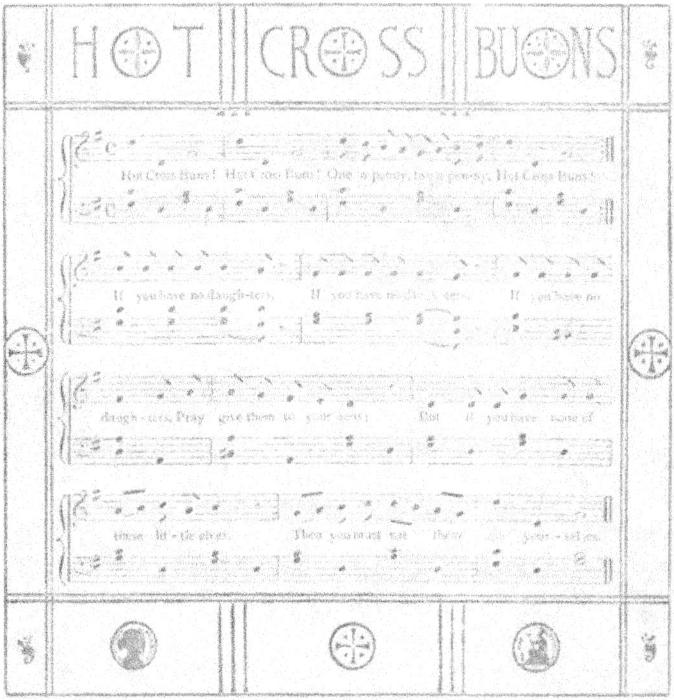
HOT CROSS BUNS

THE · LITTLE · WOMAN

'AND·THE·PEDLAR'

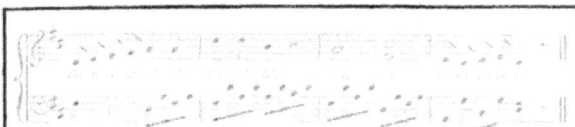

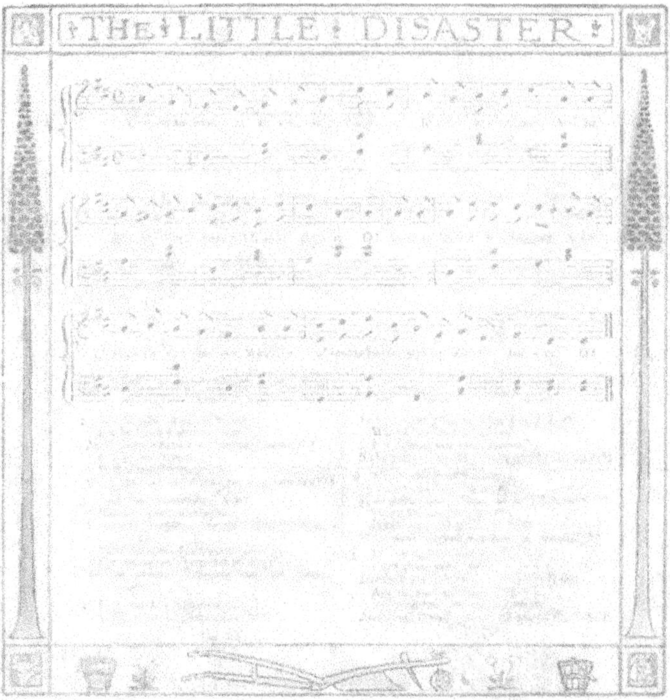
THE LITTLE DISASTER

THE OLD WOMAN OF NORWICH

There was an old wo-man and what do you think? She lived up-on nothing but vic-tuals and drink: Vic-tuals and drink were the chief of her diet, Yet this plaguey old wo-man could ne-ver be quiet.

THE OLD WOMAN
TOSSED UP IN A BLANKET

BUY A BROOM

From Deutsch-land I come with my light wares all la - den, To door - happy England in summer's gay bloom; Then la - ten, fair la - dy, gay youth or sweet maiden, Come buy of the wan-der-ing Bavar - i - a broom, A large one to sell the la - dy, and a small one for the ba - by. O buy a pretty broom, good la - dy, come buy of a bee-om.

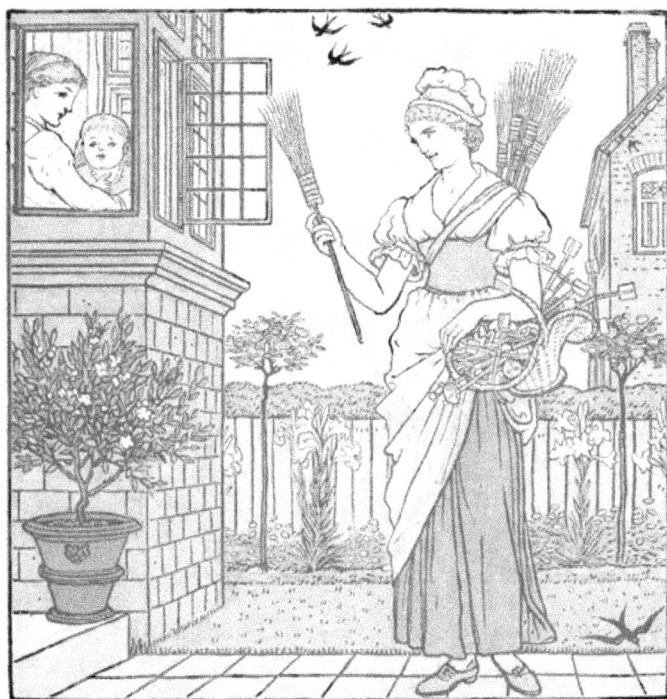

HAUSEGESINDE

Wi - de - wi - de - wen - ne heisst mei - ne Trut - hen - ne,

Kann - nicht - ruhn heisst mein Huhn. We - del - schwanz heisst mei - ne Gans;

Wi - de - wi - de - wen - ne heisst mei - ne Trut - hen - ne.

2 Widewidewenne heisst meine Trut-henne,
Entequent heisst meine Ent,
Sammetpratz heisst meine Katz;
Widewidewenne heisst meine Trut-henne.

3 Widewidewenne heisst meine Trut-henne,
Schwarz und weiss heisst meine Geiss,
Schmartfpflein heisst mein Schwein;
Widewidewenne heisst meine Trut-henne.

SCHLAF,
KINDLEIN, SCHLAF.
Schlaf, Kind-lein, schlaf, Drau-ssen steht ein
Schaf, Stösst sich an ein-em Stein-e-lein. Thut ihm weh das
Bein-e-lein. Schlaf, Kindlein, schlaf, Schlaf, Kindlein, schlaf.

THE JOLLY TESTER

O dear Six-pence, I've got Six-pence, I love Six-pence as
I love my life; I'll spend a pen-ny on't, and
I'll lend an-o-ther on't, And I'll car-ry four-pence home to my wife.

2 O dear Four-pence, I've got Four-pence,
I love Four-pence as I love my life;
I'll spend a penny on't, and I'll lend an-
other on't,
And I'll carry two-pence home to my wife.

3 O dear Two-pence, I've got Two-pence,
I love Two-pence as I love my life;
I'll spend a penny on't, and I'll lend a penny
on't,
And I'll carry nothing home to my wife.

4 O dear nothing, I've got nothing,
What will nothing buy for my wife?
I have nothing, I spend nothing,
I love nothing better than my wife.

LUCY ~ LOCKET

THE·LITTLE·COCK·SPARROW

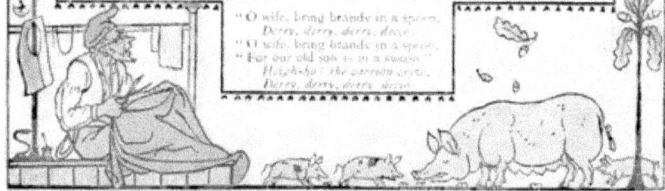

THE CARRION CROW

A car-rion crow sat on an oak, Der-ry, der-ry, der-ry,
der-ry; A car-rion crow sat on an oak, Watching a tai-lor
shaping his cloak. Heigh-ho! the car-rion crow, Derry, derry, der-ry, der-ro.

2 "O wife, bring me my old bent bow."
   Derry, derry, derry, derro;
   "O wife, bring me my old bent bow,
   "That I may shoot you carrion crow."
   Heigh-ho! the carrion crow,
   Derry, derry, derry, derro.

3 The tailor shot, and he missed his mark,
   Derry, derry, derry, derro;
   The tailor shot, and he missed his mark,
   And shot his old sow right through the heart.
   Heigh-ho! the carrion crow,
   Derry, derry, derry, derro.

   "O wife, bring brandy in a spoon,
   Derry, derry, derry, derro;
   "O wife, bring brandy in a spoon,
   "For our old sow is in a swoon."
   Heigh-ho! the carrion crow,
   Derry, derry, derry, derro.

THE·SCARECROW

O all you big black crows, how I don't you eat my

the the crops, While I lie down to take a nap. Shoo

O Shoo O

2 If father be perchance abed I come,
With his cocked hat and his two guns;
Then you must fly, and I must fall,
Shoo O! Shoo O!

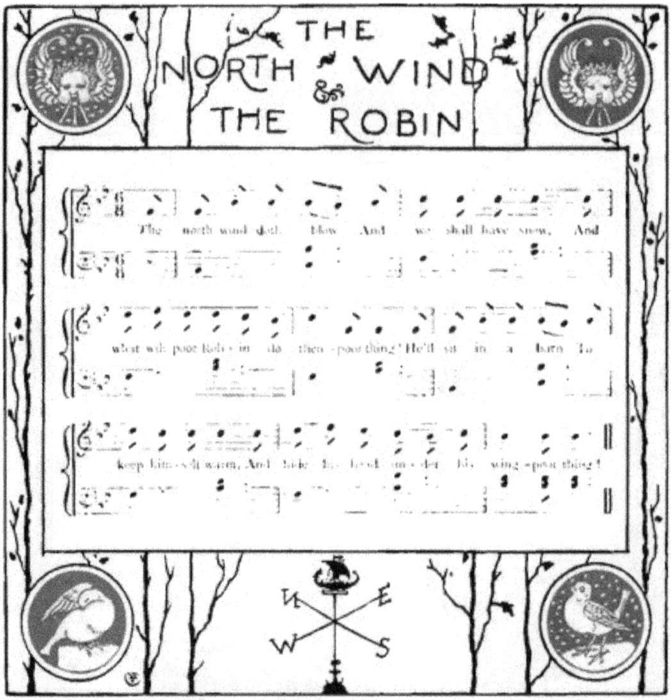
THE
NORTH WIND
&
THE ROBIN
E
W
S

ABC
A. B. C, die Kat - ze lief im Schnee, Und
je - mi-ne, O je - mi-ne, O je - mi-ne, O je!

ET·MOI·DE·MEN·COURIR·

En passant d'nou un p'tit bois, Où le cou-cou chan-toit, Où le cou-
cou, chan-toit; Dans son jo - li chant il di - sait; Coucou, cou-cou, cou-cou, cou-
cou, Et moi qui croy-ais qu'il di - sait; Cass'lui le cou, cou-lui le
cou! Et moi de m'en cour', cour, cour, Et moi de m'en cou - rir!

2 En passant auprès d'un étang
   Où les canards chantoient,
   Où les canards chantoient
   Dans leur joli chant ils disoient;
   "Cancan, cancan, cancan, cancan,"
   Et moi qui croyais qu'ils disoient;
   "Jett'le dedans, jett'le dedans,"
   Et moi de m'en cour', cour', cour',
   Et moi de m'en courir!

3 En passant devant une maison,
   Où la bonne femm' chantoit,
   Où la bonne femm' chantoit
   Dans son joli chant ell' disait;
   "Dodo, dodo, dodo, dodo,"
   Et moi qui croyais qu'ell' disait;
   "Cass'lui les os, cass'lui les os,"
   Et moi de m'en cour', cour', cour',
   Et moi de m'en courir!

AIKEN·DRUM

1. There was a man lived in the moon, lived in the moon, lived in the moon, There was a man lived in the moon, And his name was Ai - kin Drum, And he played up - on a la - dle, a la - dle, a la - dle, And he played up - on a la - dle, And his name was Aikin Drum.

2 And his hat was made of good cream cheese,
And his name, &c.

3 And his coat was made of good roast beef,
And his name, &c.

4 And his buttons were made of penny loaves,
And his name, &c.

5 His waistcoat was made of crust of pies,
And his name, &c.

6 His breeches were made of haggis bags,
And his name, &c.

7 There was a man in another town,
And his name was Willy Wood;

And he played upon a razor,
And his name was Willy Wood.

8 And he ate up all the good cream cheese,
And his name, &c.

9 And he ate up all the good roast beef,
And his name, &c.

10 And he ate up all the penny loaves,
And his name, &c.

11 And he ate up all the good pie crust,
And his name, &c.

12 But he choked upon the haggis bags,
And there was an end of Willy Wood.

BILLY ⚜ PRINGLE ⚜

Bil-ly Prin-gle had a lit-tle pig, When it was young it was not ver-y big,

When it was old it lived in clover, Now it's dead and that will a-over. Bil-ly Pringle

he lay down and died, Bet-ty Prin-gle she lay down and cried, So there was an end of

one, two, and three, Billy Pringle he, Betty Pringle she, and the piggy wiggy hee.

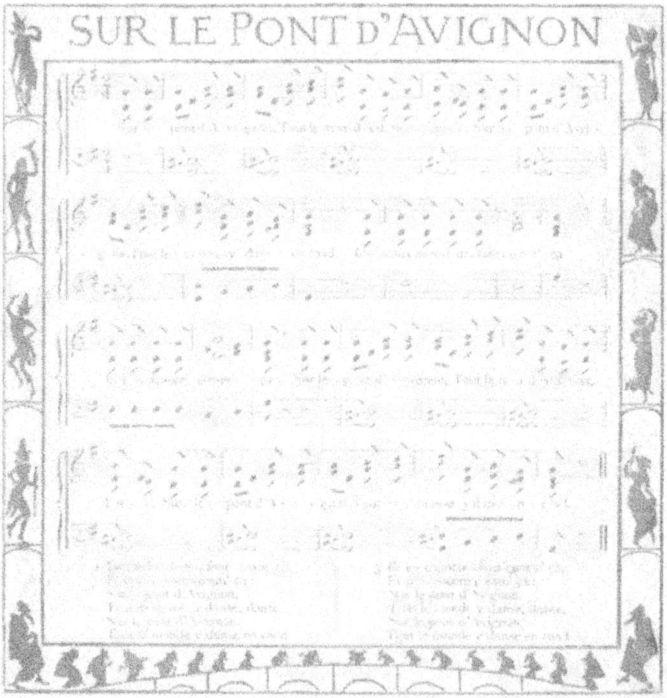
SUR LE PONT D'AVIGNON

CHARLEY OVER THE WATER

Over the water and over the sea, And over the water to
Charley; And Charley loves good ale and wine, And Charley loves good
brandy, And Charley loves a pretty girl As sweet as sugar candy.

Over the water and over the sea,
And over the water to Charley;
I'll have none of your nasty beef,
Nor I'll have none of your barley;
But I'll have some of your very best flour
To make a white cake for my Charley.

THE·THREE · LITTLE·KITTENS

There were three little kittens Put on their mittens To eat some

Christmas pie. Mew, mew, Mew, mew, Mew, mew, mew.

2 These three little kittens
They lost their mittens,
And all began to cry.
Mew, mew, &c.

3 "Go, go, naughty kittens,
"And find your mittens,
"Or you shan't have any pie."
Mew, mew, &c.

4 These three little kittens
They found their mittens,
And joyfully they did cry.
Mew, mew, &c.

5 "O Granny, dear!
"Our mittens are here,
"Make haste and cut up the pie!"
Purrrrr, prrrrrr, prrrrrrr.

PUSSY CAT

Pus - sy - cat high,   Pus - sy - cat low,

Pus - sy - cat was a fine ten - or of tow.

2 Pussycat slept into the barn,
   With her bag-pipes under her arm.

3 And then she told a tale to me,
   How Mousey had married a humble-bee.

4 Then was I ever so glad,
   That Mousey had married so clever a lad.

119

ZWEI HASEN

Zwischen Berg und tie-fen, tie-fen Thal, Sas-sen einst zwei Ha-sen.

Fras-sen ab das grü-ne, grü-ne Gras, Frassen ab das grü-ne, grü-ne Gras

Bis auf den Ra-sen. Bis... auf den Ra-sen.

2. Als sie satt gefressen, 'fressen war'n,
Setzten sie sich nieder,
Bis nun dann der Jäger, Jäger kam,
Und schoss sie nieder, und schoss sie nieder.

3. Als sie sich nun angesammelt hatt'n
Und sich besannen.
Dass sie noch Leben, Leben hatt'n
Liefen sie von dannen.

120

LA BERGÈRE

Il é-tait un' ber-gè-re, Et ron, ron, ron, pe-tit pa-ta-pon; Il é-tait
un' ber-gè-re, Qui gar-dait ses moutons, Ron, ron, Qui gar-dait ses mou-tons.

1. Elle fit un fromage,
   Et ron, ron, ron, petit patapon;
   Elle fit un fromage,
   Du lait de ses moutons,
   Ron, ron,
   Du lait de ses moutons.

3. Le chat qui la regarde,
   Et ron, ron, ron, petit patapon;
   Le chat qui la regarde
   D'un petit air felpon,
   Ron, ron,
   D'un petit air felpon.

4. Si tu y mets la patte,
   Et ron, ron, ron, petit patapon,
   Si tu y mets la patte,
   Tu auras du bâton,
   Ron, ron,
   Tu auras du bâton.

5. Il n'y mit pas la patte,
   Et ron, ron, ron, petit patapon;
   Il n'y mit pas la patte,
   Il y met le menton,
   Ron, ron,
   Il y mit le menton.

LE·PETIT·CHASSEUR

LOOBY LIGHT

Now we dance loo - by, loo - by, loo - by, Now we dance loo -by, loo - by light;

Now we dance loo - by, loo - by, loo - by, Now we dance looby as yes - ter - night.

Shake your right hand a lit-tle, Shake your left hand a lit-tle.

Shake your head a lit-tle, And turn you round a - bout.

See - saw Margery Daw Sold her
bed to lie up-on straw. Was - n't she a
nas - ty slut To sell her bed and lie up-on dirt?

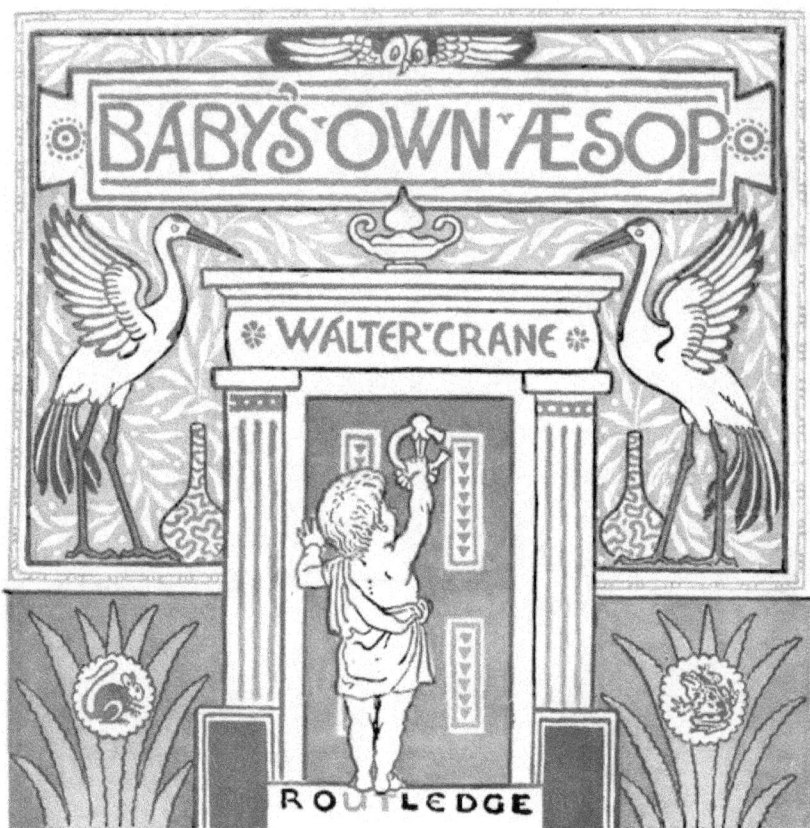

BABY'S OWN ÆSOP

WALTER CRANE

ROUTLEDGE

BABY'S·OWN·ÆSOP

WALTER·CRANE

ALSO BY THE
SAME:

"THE
BABY'S
OPERA"

&
THE
BABY'S
BOUQUET"

ENGRAVED & PRINTED
IN COLOURS BY
EDMUND·EVANS

ROUTLEDGE

134

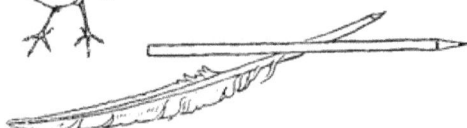

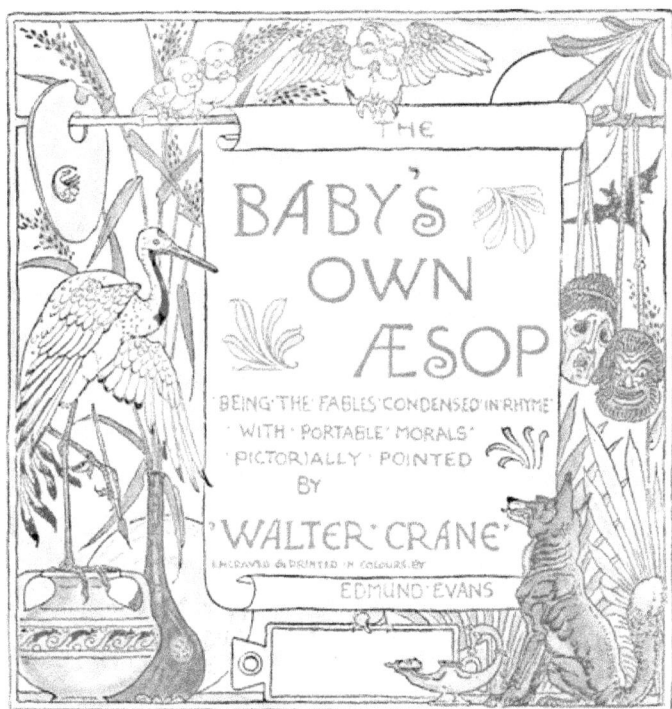

THE
BABY'S
OWN
ÆSOP

BEING·THE·FABLES·CONDENSED·IN·RHYME
·WITH·PORTABLE·MORALS·
·PICTORIALLY·POINTED·
BY

·WALTER·CRANE·

ENGRAVED·&·PRINTED·IN·COLOURS·BY
EDMUND·EVANS

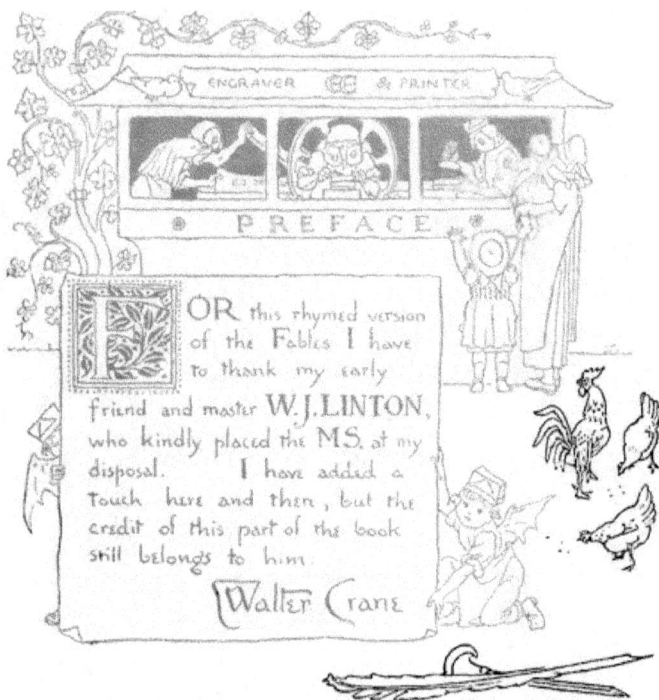

ENGRAVER & PRINTER

P R E F A C E

FOR this rhymed version of the Fables I have to thank my early friend and master W.J. LINTON, who kindly placed the M.S. at my disposal. I have added a touch here and then, but the credit of this part of the book still belongs to him.

Walter Crane

To the
Possessors of
& "Baby's Opera"
"Baby's Bouquet"
with
Walter Crane's
Compliments

THE BABY'S BOUQUET
THE BABY'S OPERA

CONTENTS

THE FOX & THE GRAPES

THIS Fox has a longing
for grapes,
He jumps, but the bunch still
escapes.
So he goes away sour,
And, 'tis said, to this hour
Declares that he's no taste
for grapes.

"THE GRAPES OF DISAPPOINTMENT ARE ALWAYS SOUR."

THE COCK & THE PEARL

A ROOSTER, while scratching
for grain,
Found a Pearl. He just paused to
explain
That a jewel's no good
To a fowl wanting food,
And then kicked it aside with
disdain.

"IF HE ASK BREAD WILL YE GIVE HIM A STONE?"

THE WOLF AND THE LAMB

A WOLF, wanting lamb for his
dinner,
Growled out "Lamb you wronged me,
you sinner;"
Bleated Lamb "Nay, not true!"
Answered Wolf "Then 't was Ewe.
Ewe or lamb, you will serve for my
dinner."

FRAUD AND VIOLENCE HAVE NO SCRUPLES

THE·WIND·&·THE·SUN

THE WIND and the Sun had a bet,
The wayfarers' cloak which should get:
Blew the Wind — the cloak clung;
Shone the Sun — the cloak flung,
Showed the Sun had the best of it yet.

·TRUE·STRENGTH·IS·NOT·BLUSTER·

KING·LOG·&·KING·STORK·

THE FROGS prayed to
        Jove for a King:
"Not a log, but a livelier
              thing."
Jove sent them a Stork,
Who did royal work,
For he gobbled them up, did
            their king.

DON'T·HAVE·KINGS

144

THE FRIGHTENED LION

A BULL FROG, according
to rule,
Sat a-croak in his
usual pool
And he laughed in his heart
As a Lion did start
In a fright from the brink
like a fool.

"IMAGINARY FEARS ARE THE WORST"

THE·MOUSE·& THE·LION

A POOR thing the Mouse
was, and yet,
When the Lion got
caught in a net,
All his strength was no use
'Twas the poor little Mouse
Who nibbled him out of the
net.

SMALL·CAUSES·MAY·PRODUCE·GREAT·RESULTS

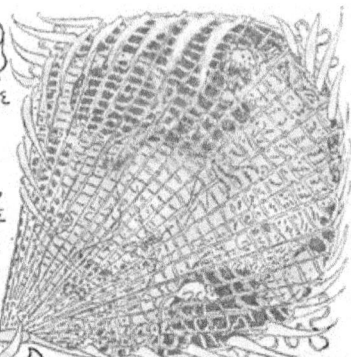

THE·MARRIED·MOUSE

SO the Mouse had Miss
Lion for bride;
Very great was his joy and
his pride:
But it chanced that she put
On her husband her foot,
And the weight was too much,
So he died

·ONE·MAY·BE·TOO·AMBITIOUS·

HERCULES & THE WAGGONER

WHEN the God saw the
Waggoner kneel,
Crying "Hercules! Lift me
my wheel,
From the mud, where 'tis stuck!
He laughed — "No such luck;
Set your shoulder yourself
To the wheel.'

THE GODS HELP THOSE WHO HELP THEMSELVES

THE·LAZY·HOUSEMAIDS

TWO Maids killed the
Rooster whose warning
Awoke them too soon every
morning:
But small were their gains,
For their Mistress took pains
To rouse them herself without
warning.

·LAZINESS·IS·ITS·OWN·PUNISHMENT·

THE SNAKE & THE FILE

A SNAKE, in a fix, tried
a File
For a dinner. "'Tis not worth
your while,"
Said the steel, "don't mistake;
I'm accustomed to take;
To give's not the way of
a File."

WE·MAY·MEET·OUR·MATCH

THE FOX & THE CROW

SAID sly Fox to the Crow
with the cheese,
"Let me hear your sweet voice,
now, do please!"
And this Crow, being weak,
Cawed the bit from her beak.
"Music charms", said the Fox,
"and here's cheese!"

: BEWARE · OF · FLATTERERS :

THE DOG IN THE MANGER

A COW sought a mouth-
ful of hay;
But a Dog in the man-
ger there lay,
And he snapped out "how now?"
When most mildly, the Cow
Adventured a morsel to pray.

· DON'T · BE · SELFISH ·

THE FROG & THE BULL

SAID the Frog, quite puffed
up to the eyes,
"Was this Bull about me
as to size?"
"Rather bigger, frog-brother,"
"Puff, puff," said the other,
"A Frog is a Bull if he
tries!"

· BRAG · IS · NOT · ALWAYS · BELIEF ·

THE FOX & THE CRANE

YOU have heard how Sir
        Fox treated Crane:
With soup in a plate. When again
    They dined, a long bottle
    Just suited Crane's throttle;
And Sir Fox licked the outside
                in vain.

THERE · ARE · GAMES · THAT · TWO · CAN
            PLAY · AT ·

HORSE AND MAN

WHEN the Horse first
took Man on his back,
To help him the Stag to attack;
How little his dread,
As the enemy fled,
Man would make him his
slave & his hack.

· ADVANTAGES · MAY · BE · DEARLY · BOUGHT ·

THE ASS & THE ENEMY

"GET up! let us flee from
the Foe,"
Said the Man: but the Ass
said. "Why so?"
"Will they double my load,
Or my blows? Then, by Goad,
And by stirrup, I've no cause
to go."

· YOUR · REASONS · ARE ·
NOT · MINE ·

THE·FOX·&·THE·MOSQUITOES

BEING plagued with Mosquitoes
   one day
Said old Fox: "pray don't send
            them away,
For a hungrier swarm
Would work me more harm;"
I had rather the full ones
            should stay."

'THERE·WERE·POLITICIANS·IN·ÆSOP'S·TIME'

THE·FOX·&·THE·LION

THE first time the Fox
         had a sight
Of the Lion, he 'most died
         of fright;
When he next met his eye,
Fox felt just a bit shy;
But the next - quite at ease,
         & polite.

'FAMILIARITY·DESTROYS·FEAR'·

THE MISER & HIS GOLD

HE buried his Gold in a hole.
One saw, and the treasure
he stole.
Said another, "What matter?
Don't raise such a clatter,
You can still go & sit by
The hole."

USE ALONE GIVES VALUE

THE GOLDEN EGGS

A GOLDEN egg, one every
day,
That simpleton's Goose
used to lay;
So he killed the poor thing,
Swifter fortune to bring,
And dined off his fortune
That day.

GREED OVEREACHES ITSELF

THE MAN THAT PLEASED NONE

THROUGH the town
this good Man & his Son
Strove to ride as to please every one:
Self, Son, or both tried,
Then the Ass had a ride;
While the world, at their efforts,
poked fun.

YOU CANNOT HOPE TO PLEASE ALL DON'T TRY

THE OAK & THE REEDS

GIANT Oak, in his
    strength & his scorn
Of the winds, by the roots
            was uptorn:
But slim Reeds at his side,
The fierce gale did outride,
Since, by bending the burden
                was borne.

: BEND. NOT BREAK :

THE FIR & THE BRAMBLE

THE Fir-tree looked down
        on the Bramble.
"Poor thing, only able to scramble
About on the ground."
        Just then an 'axe' sound
Made the Fir wish himself
            but a Bramble.

: PRIDE OF PLACE HAS ITS DISADVANTAGES :

THE·HART·&·THE·VINE

A Hart by the hunters pur-
sued,
Safely hid in a Vine, 'till
he chewed
The sweet tender green,
And, through shaking leaves
seen,
He was slain by his ingratitude.

SPARE·YOUR·BENEFACTORS

THE·MAN·&·THE·SNAKE·

IN pity he brought the poor
         Snake,
To be warmed at his fire.
          A mistake!
  For the ungrateful thing
  Wife & children would sting.
I have known some as bad as
          the Snake.

"BEWARE HOW YOU"

"ENTERTAIN TRAITORS"

"THE·ASS·IN·THE·LION'S·SKIN

WHAT pranks I
shall play!" thought
the Ass,
In this skin for a Lion to pass;"
But he left one ear out,
And a hiding, no doubt,
"Lion" had – on the skin of
an Ass!

· IMPOSTORS ·
GENERALLY · FORGET ·
· SOMETHING ·

:THE·LION·&·THE·STATVE:

On a Statue - King Lion
                dethroned,
  Showing conqueror Man,—
              Lion frowned.
"If a Lion, you know,
  Had been sculptor, he'd show
Lion rampant, and Man on the
              ground."

THE·STORY·DEPENDS·ON·THE·TELLER·

THE BOASTER

IN the house, in the market, the streets,
Everywhere he was boasting his feats;
    Till one said, with a sneer,
    "Let us see it done here!
What's so oft done with ease, one repeats."

· DEEDS · NOT · WORDS ·

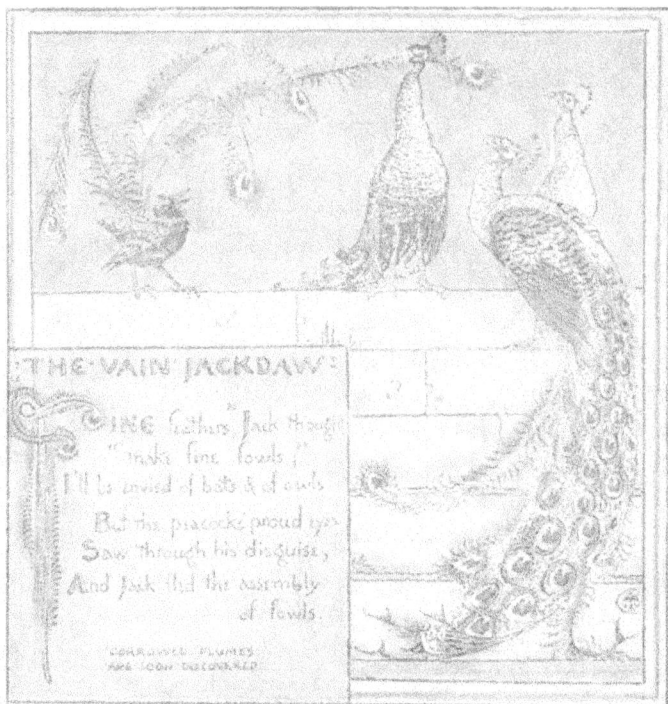

THE VAIN JACKDAW

FINE feathers Jack thought
"make fine fowls;"
I'll be envied of bats & of owls
But the peacocks proud eyes
Saw through his disguise,
And Jack fled the assembly
of fowls.

BORROWED PLUMES
ARE SOON DISCOVERED

THE PEACOCK'S COMPLAINT

THE Peacock con-
:sidered it wrong
That he had not the nightingale's
song;
So to Juno he went,
She replied, "Be content
With thy having, & hold thy
fool's tongue!"

DO NOT QUARREL WITH NATURE.

THE TWO JARS

NEVER fear! said the Brass
                    to the Glass
Of two jars that the flood
                    bore away:
"Keep you close to my side!"
But the porcelain replied,
"I'll be smashed if beside you
                    I stay."

'OUR FRIEND OUR ENEMY'

THE TWO CRABS

"So awkward, so shambling
                    a gait!"
Mrs Crab did her daughter
                    berate,
Who rejoined, "It is true
I am backward; but you
Needed lessons in walking
                    quite late."

'LOOK AT HOME'

BROTHER & SISTER

TWIN children: the Girl,
                     she was plain;
The Brother was handsome &
                          vain;
"Let him brag of his looks,"
   Father said; mind your books!
The best beauty is bred in the brain"

HANDSOME IS AS HANDSOME DOES

THE FOX WITHOUT A TAIL

Said Fox, minus tail in a trap,
"My friends! here's a lucky
mishap;
Give your tails a short lease!"
- But the foxes weren't geese,
And none followed the fashion
of trap.

YET·SOME·FASHIONS·HAVE·NO
BETTER·REASON·

The DOG & the Shadow

HIS image the Dog did not
know,
Or his bone's, in the pond's
painted show.
"T'other dog", so he thought
"Has got more than he ought";
So he snapped, & his dinner
saw go.

GREED IS SOMETIMES
CAUGHT BY ITS
OWN BAIT

THE CROW & THE PITCHER

HOW the cunning old
Crow got his drink
When 'twas low in the
    pitcher, just think!
Don't say that he spilled it!
With pebbles he filled it,
'Till the water rose up to
        the brink.

· USE · YOUR · WITS ·

THE · EAGLE · AND · THE · CROW

THE Eagle flew off with a lamb;
  Then the Crow thought to lift an old ram,
    In his eaglish conceit,
      The wool tangled his feet,
And the shepherd laid hold of the sham.

: BEWARE OF OVERRATING YOUR OWN POWERS :

THE·BLIND·DOE·

A poor half-blind Doe her one eye
kept shoreward, all danger to spy,
    As she fed by the sea,
    Poor innocent! she
Was shot from a boat passing by.

: WATCH · ON · ALL · SIDES :

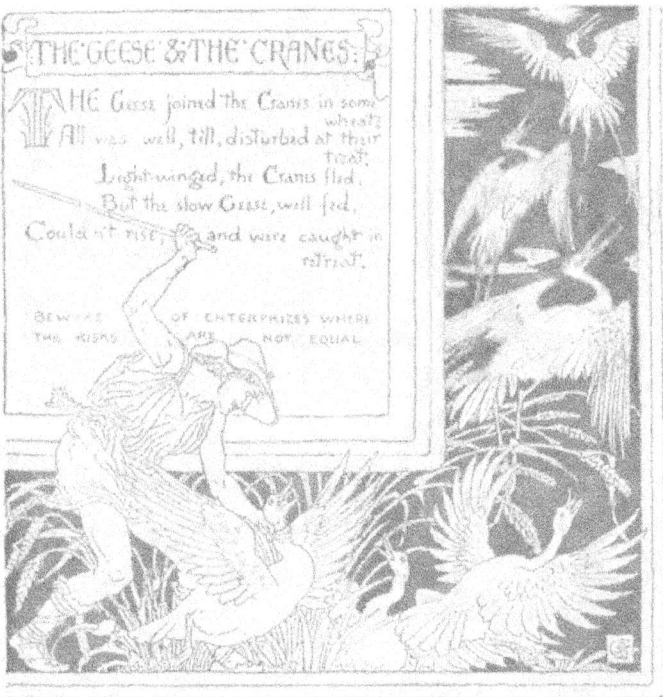

THE·GEESE·&·THE·CRANES·

THE Geese joined the Cranes in some
        wheat;
All was well, till, disturbed at their
        treat,
    Light-winged, the Cranes fled:
    But the slow Geese, well fed,
Couldn't rise, and were caught in
        retreat.

BEWARE OF ENTERPRIZES WHERE
THE RISKS ARE NOT EQUAL

THE·TRUMPETER·TAKEN·PRISONER

A Trumpeter, prisoner made,
Hoped his life would be spared
He'd no part in the fight,
But they answered him-Right,
But what of the music you made?"

SONGS MAY SERVE
CAUSE AS WELL AS SWORD

HOT AND COLD:

WHEN to warm his cold fingers
man blew,
And again, but to cool the hot stew;
Simple Satyr, unused
To man's ways, felt confused,
When the same mouth blew hot &
cold too!

ÆSOP·AIMED·AT·DOUBLE·DEALING·

174

NEITHER·BEAST·NOR·BIRD.

A Beast he
would be, or
a bird,
As might suit, thought the Bat:
but he erred.
When the battle was done,
He found that no one
Would take him for friend at
his word.

"BETWEEN·TWO·STOOLS
YOU·MAY·COME·TO·THE·GROUND"

THE STAG IN THE OX-STALL & THE DEER & THE LION

SAFE enough lay the poor
        hunted Deer
  In the ox-stall, with nothing
        to fear
From the careless-eyed men:
  Till the Master came; then
There was no hiding-place
    for the Deer.

FROM the hounds the swift
      Deer sped away,
To his cave, where in past times
        he lay
Well concealed; unaware
  Of a Lion couched there,
For a spring that soon made
    him his prey.

AN EYE IS
KEEN IN ITS
OWN
INTEREST

FATE
CAN MEET
AS WELL AS
FOLLOW

'THE LION IN LOVE'

THOUGH the Lion in love let
                 them draw
All his teeth, and pare down every
                          claw,
He'd no bride for his pains,
For they beat out his brains
Ere he sat on his maiden
    a paw.

OUR VERY MEANS MAY DEFEAT OUR ENDS

177

THE·CAT·AND·VENVS

MIGHT his Cat be a woman", he said:
Venus changed her: the couple were wed:
But a mouse in her sight
Metamorphosed her quite,
And, for bride, a cat found he instead.

: NATURE· WILL· OUT :

MICE·IN·COUNCIL:

AGAINST Cat sat
a Council of Mice.
Every Mouse came out
prompt with advice
And a bell on Cat's throat
Would have met a round vote
Had the bell-hanger not
been so nice.

: THE· BEST· POLICY· OFTEN·
TURNS· ON· AN· IF : :

·THE·HEN·AND·THE·FOX·

THE Hen roosted high on her
perch;
Hungry Fox down below, on the
search,
  Coaxed her hard to descend
  She replied, "Most dear friend!
I feel more secure on my perch "

BEWARE OF INTERESTED FRIENDSHIPS!

·THE·CAT·AND·THE·FOX·

THE Fox said "I can play,
when it fits,
Many wiles that with man make
me quits "
  "**B**ut my trick's up a tree!"
  Said the Cat, safe to see
Clever Fox hunted out of his wits

TRUST TO SKILL RATHER THAN WIT

THE·HARE·AND·THE·TORTOISE·

'TWAS a race between Tortoise and Hare,
Puss was sure she'd so much time to spare,
    That she lay down to sleep,
    And let old Thick-shell creep
To the winning-post first. You may stare.

PERSISTENCE BEATS IMPULSE!

THE·HARES·AND·THE·FROGS·

TIMID Hares, from the trumpeting wind,
Fled as swift as the fear in their mind;
    Till in fright from their fear,
    From the green sedges near,
Leaping Frogs left their terror behind.

'OUR·OWN' ARE NOT·THE·ONLY·TROUBLES'

PORCUPINE, SNAKE, & COMPANY.

GOING shares with the Snakes, Porcu-
       pine
Said "the best of the bargain is mine!"
Nor would he back down,
When the snakes would disown
The agreement his quills made them
                                sign.

· HASTY · PARTNERSHIPS · MAY · BE · REPENTED · OF ·

THE · BEAR · & · THE · BEES.

THEIR honey I'll have when I
                          please;
"Who cares for such small things as
                          Bees?"
Said the Bear; but the stings
Of these very small things
Left him not very much at his ease.

THE · WEAKEST UNITED MAY BE STRONG TO AVENGE

THE BUNDLE OF STICKS

To his sons, who fell out, father
                         spake:
"This Bundle of Sticks you can't
                         break;"
Take them singly, with ease,
You may break as you please;
So, dissension your strength will
                         unmake.

STRENGTH IS IN UNITY.

THE FARMER'S TREASURE

DIG deeply, my Sons! through this field!
There's a Treasure — he died:
untrevealed
The spot where 'twas laid,
They dug as he bade;

And the Treasure was found in
the yield.

PRODUCTIVE LABOUR IS THE ONLY SOURCE OF WEALTH

181

:THE·COCK·THE·ASS·&·THE·LION:

THE Ass gave a horrible bray,
  Cock crowed; Lion scamper'd away,
    Ass judged he was scared
    By the bray, and so dared
To pursue; Lion ate him they say.

DON'T TAKE ALL THE CREDIT TO YOURSELF.

:THE·ASS·AND·THE·LAP·DOG:

"HOW Master that little Dog pris?"
  Thinks the Ass; & with jealousy frisk,
    So he climbs Master's knees,
    Hoping dog-like to please,
And a drubbing is all that he gets.

ASSES MUST NOT EXPECT TO BE FONDLED.

:FORTVNE·AND·THE·BOY:

A Boy heedless slept by the well
By Dame Fortune awaked; truth to tell.
Said she "Hadst been drowned,
'T would have surely been found'
This by Fortune, not Folly befel."

FORTUNE IS NOT ANSWERABLE FOR OUR WANT OF FORESIGHT

THE·UNGRATEFUL·WOLF:

TO the Wolf, from whose throat Dr Crane
Drew the bone, his long bill made
it plain
He expected his fee:
Snarled Wolf—"fiddle de dee,
Be thankful your head's out again"

:SOME·CHARACTERS·
HAVE·NO·SENSE·OF·OBLIGATION:

:THE·FISHERMAN·&·THE·FISH:

PRAYED the Fish, as the Fisherman took
Him, a poor little mite, from his hook,
"Let me go! I'm so small."
He replied, "Not at all!
You're the biggest, perhaps in the brook."

:·A·LITTLE·CERTAINTY·IS·BETTER·THAN·A·GREAT·CHANCE·:

THE·HERDSMAN'S·VOWS

A KID vowed to Jove, so might he
Find his herd, & his herd did
Soon, of lions the prey;
Then 'twas:- "Get me away,
And a goat of the best take for ,,

HOW OFTEN WOULD WE MEND OUR WORSE!

THE·HORSE·AND·THE·ASS·

O VERLADEN the Ass was, the Horse
Would n't help, but had time for to
When the Ass lay dead there, Horse
For he then had to bear
Both the load of the Ass &his
CORSE.

GRUDGE·NOT·HELP!

187

THE·ASS·&·THE·SICK·LION:

CRAFTY Lion,—perhaps with the gout
Kept his cave; where, to solve any doubt,
    Many visitors go:
    But the Ass, he said "No!
They go in, but I've seen none come out."
    ·REASON·FROM·RESULTS·

·THE·END·

PRINTED
BY
EDMUND
EVANS

BOUND
BY
LEIGHTON
SON &
HODGE